TORNADOES

DISASTERS

Merrilee Hooker

The Rourke Corporation, Inc.
Vero Beach, Florida 32964

Edited by Sandra A. Robinson

PHOTO CREDITS
© Emil Punter: title page, p. 8, 12, 13, 17, 18; © Lynn M. Stone: p. 7;
© Wyman Meinzer: p. 4, 15; courtesy of NOAA: cover; courtesy of
NASA: p. 10, 21

Library of Congress Cataloging-in-Publication Data

Hooker, Merrilee, 1955-
    Tornadoes / by Merrilee Hooker.
    p. cm. — (Discovery library of disasters)
    Includes index.
    Summary: Discusses how tornadoes begin and work, some of
the strange things they have done, and advice for protecting
oneself during a tornado.
    ISBN 0-86593-248-4
    1. Tornadoes—Juvenile literature. [1. Tornadoes.] I. Title.
II. Series.
QC955.2.H66 1993
551.55'3—dc20
                                             92-41101
                                               CIP
                                             AC

Printed in the USA

TABLE OF CONTENTS

TORNADOES

A tornado is a brief, but powerful whirling windstorm. It forms a dark, funnel-shaped cloud that is one of nature's most powerful forces. A tornado can cause **disaster**—terrible loss of lives and damage to property.

Tornadoes are often called "twisters" because of their whirling motion. The tornado cloud itself usually travels about 45 miles per hour. The violent winds within the tornado are probably traveling hundreds of miles per hour.

A tornado twists across the plains of Texas in "Tornado Alley, U.S.A."

HOW A TORNADO BEGINS

Strong thunderstorms on warm, humid days create the conditions that allow tornadoes to form. A tornado may develop within a thunderstorm when warm, wet air from one direction and cold, dry air from another bump into each other.

Rumbling loudly, a tornado usually carries heavy rain, thunder, lightning and **hail.** Hail is made up of ice balls. They may be pea-sized or as large as golf balls.

Tornadoes can form—and vanish—very quickly.

Under the right conditions, tornadoes develop in thunderstorms

HOW TORNADOES WORK

A tornado funnel cloud rises and dips, almost as if it is a snake reaching down from the sky. The tornado is fairly harmless until it touches the ground. With each touchdown, the storm rips a path of destruction. The path of a typical tornado is less than 100 yards across and a mile long.

A tornado works like a big vacuum cleaner. It sucks objects off the ground. As it spins with tremendous force, it can destroy trees, buildings, cars and anything else in its path.

Twenty-five people died in the terrible path of a tornado that struck Plainfield, Illinois, an August 28, 1990

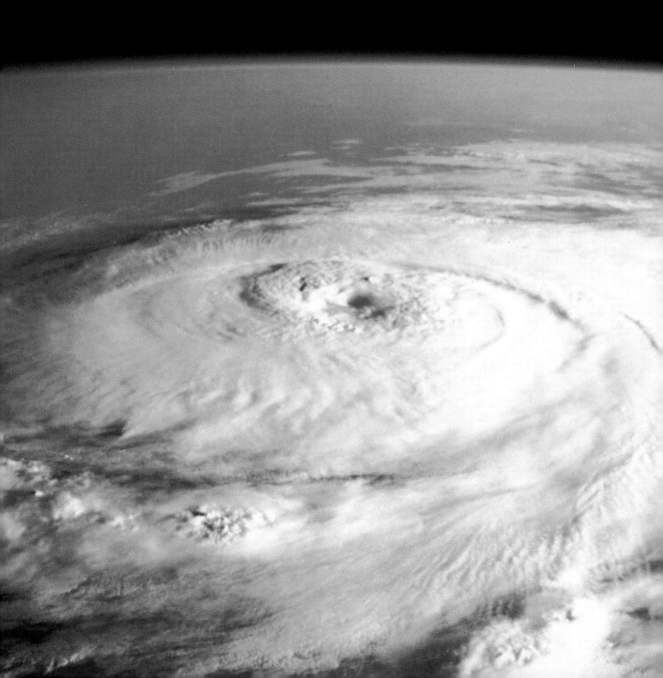

TORNADOES AND HURRICANES

Tornadoes are the most violent of storms. They also have the shortest lifespan. A tornado usually lasts only 10 to 20 minutes. As weather conditions change, a tornado loses its strength quickly and disappears.

Although it is also a windstorm, a **hurricane** is less violent than a tornado. Hurricanes form over warm oceans. They last for several days and blow across an area up to 400 miles wide.

Spacecraft view of Hurricane Elena as the windstorm traveled across ocean water

Only a washer and dryer escaped the tornado's fury in this neighborhood

Much of this high school was destroyed when a tornado struck

WHEN AND WHERE TORNADOES STRIKE

Tornadoes in North America usually form during the late spring and early summer. Tornadoes can occur anywhere, but most develop over the flat lands of the Midwest.

The level ground of Texas, Oklahoma, Kansas and Missouri has been nicknamed "Tornado Alley." Most of the 700 tornadoes recorded each year in the United States strike the Tornado Alley states.

Tornadoes that form over water are called **waterspouts.**

Violent thunderstorms, like this one in Texas, can unleash tornadoes

TORNADO DISASTERS

Each year killer tornadoes strike the Midwest. Among them was a tornado that killed 689 people in three states in March, 1925. It was the worst tornado in United States history.

Late one afternoon in August, 1990, with little warning, a killer tornado slashed into Plainfield, Illinois. Most of Plainfield High School was destroyed by the twister. Fortunately, school was not in session. Student athletes on the school's practice fields found safety inside the school in a room below ground level.

Plainfield High School after it was battered by a tornado

THE TORNADO'S TOUCH

The power of a tornado can do strange things, such as driving a straw through a board. A tornado in France sucked up a pond. Miles away, the tornado released a "rain" of frogs and fish.

A tornado in Italy lifted a sleeping baby. She was still asleep when the tornado gently put her down again. In England, a tornado plucked the feathers from chickens, but did not kill the naked birds.

A Minnesota tornado lifted a train 80 feet into the air and dropped it. Unbelievably, the wreck killed only one of the 117 train passengers.

A tornado left this street sign,
but blew the house next to it away

STUDYING TORNADOES

Scientists who study weather are called **meteorologists.** Meteorologists closely watch for temperatures and thunderstorms that could create tornadoes.

The use of **radar** is important to meteorologists who track thunderstorms. Radar is a system that finds distant objects in the air, such as storms, through the use of sound waves.

Scientists are still learning how tornadoes create such violent force.

Meteorologists keep careful watch on thunderstorm activity

PROTECTING PEOPLE FROM TORNADOES

It is good advice to turn on the radio or television when strong thunderstorms begin to blacken the sky. If conditions for a tornado exist, the National Weather Service will issue a **tornado watch.** If a tornado has been spotted, the National Weather Service will issue a **tornado warning.**

A basement is the best place to find safety. Stay away from windows and outside walls. Keep a battery-powered radio on, and stay where you are until it is safe to leave.

Outdoors, lie down flat in a ditch. Cover your head with your hands.

Glossary

disaster (diz AS ter) — an event that causes a great loss of property and/or lives

hail (HALE) — balls of ice that often occur during strong thunderstorms and tornadoes

hurricane (HER uh kane) — a powerful, long-lasting windstorm that forms over a warm ocean, carries heavy rains, and has winds of at least 75 miles per hour

meteorologist (meet ee er AHL uh jist) — a scientist who studies weather

radar (RAY dar) — a system in which sound wave echoes are used to locate distant objects in the air

tornado warning (tor NAY doe WORN ing) — a report that a tornado has been sighted in the area

tornado watch (tor NAY doe WAWTSCH) — a report that conditions are right for a tornado to form in the area

waterspout (WAW ter spowt) — a tornado that occurs over water and creates a tall, spinning surge of water

INDEX